DOMINIK HASEK
The Dominator

R A N D Y   S C H U L T Z

RANDY SCHULTZ
DOMINIK HASEK
The Dominator

Sports Publishing L.L.C.
Publisher: **Peter L. Bannon**
Senior Managing Editors: **Joseph J. Bannon, Jr. and Susan M. Moyer**
Art Director: **K. Jeffrey Higgerson**

Graphic Designers: **Kenneth J. O'Brien, Kerri Baker and Christine Mohrbacher**
Cover Design: **Christine Mohrbacher**
Coordinating Editor: **Noah Amstadter**
Copy Editor: **Cynthia L. McNew**

Front cover photo:
Ryan Remiorz, AP/Wide World Photos
Back cover photo:
Bill Wippert.

ISBN: 1-58261-568-3

Printed in Canada

DEDICATION

This book is dedicated to my wife and best friend, Janet, to my daughter

and son-in-law, Karla and Scott, and to my mom and late dad, Martha and

Willard Schultz. Thank you for all your love and support.

Table of Contents

Photo by Bill Wippert

Always a family man, Dominik shares the Vezina and Hart trophies with his wife Alena and son Michael at the 1998 NHL awards dinner.

Photo by Janet Schultz

CHAPTER 1

A Czech Christmas

Dominik Hasek sits on a chair in front of his locker in the visitors' locker room at HSBC Arena in Buffalo, New York.

The 2001-2002 National Hockey League season is nearly over. His team, the Detroit Red Wings, has already clinched a playoff spot. But this is not just another game for Hasek.

It is March 10, 2002, and it is the first time the veteran goaltender has returned to the western New York city since his trade from the Buffalo Sabres to the Red Wings back in July 2001.

Several members of the Buffalo media enter the Red Wings' room and gather where Hasek is seated. After exchanging greetings, Hasek answers many questions regarding his return to Buffalo. After 15 minutes of questioning, the group disbands and begins to exit the room.

Above: Dominik sports a boxing robe given to him by Sabres trainer Jim Pizzutelli. Pizzutelli traditionally presents robes to players he sees as fighters.

Photo by Bill Wippert

Right: Dominik was one of the rare goalkeepers to earn a boxing robe from team trainer Jim Pizzutelli. Normally, only skaters earn this symbol of toughness.

Photo by Bill Wippert

One reporter remains to talk further with Hasek. Following a series of questions, the reporter asks Hasek how his Christmas was. The reporter knows how important that holiday is to the net minder.

"Without a doubt, Christmas is the best holiday of the year," Dominik says. The veteran goalie has had many memorable experiences connected with Christmas.

"In Czech, it means the entire family comes together for the holiday," remarks Dominik. "It is a very quiet and peaceful time of the year."

Hasek was born in the small Czech Republic town of Pardubice (pronounced par-doo-BEETZ-ah) on January 29, 1965.

While the Czech Republic itself is almost ten years old, its history actually dates back to the fifth century. The country comprises the historic lands of Bohemia, Moravia, and part of Silesia, and it was first occupied by the Celts.

The new state of Czechoslovakia was created in 1918 following the collapse of the Habsburg Empire. The Communists took over the country in 1948. With the collapse of Communism throughout Europe in 1989, the Czechs brought about the Velvet Revolution.

Dominik's popularity transcends age and gender. Here a young Buffalo fan waits rinkside for a glimpse of her hero.

Photo by Bill Wippert

Differences between the Czechs and Slovaks on how to form a new democratic state led to an agreement to separate in 1992. The Czech Republic was proclaimed on January 1, 1993.

"Our family would celebrate Christmas on the 24th in the evening," Hasek continues. "But it was the events leading up to that evening that kept all the children in suspense. My father would go into the family room and put all the presents under the tree. Nobody was allowed in that room all day. We were always told that we couldn't go into the room until after Santa Claus had left.

"When the time came for us to go into the room, my father would ring a bell. We would open the door to the family room, and there would be the tree, all lit with real candles. You have to remember that this was before we had electricity connected to our house. There were sparklers lit around the tree, too. It was truly a beautiful sight.

Dominik poses with son Michael at the 1997 NHL Awards, where he was presented with both the Hart and Vezina trophies.
Photo by Janet Schultz

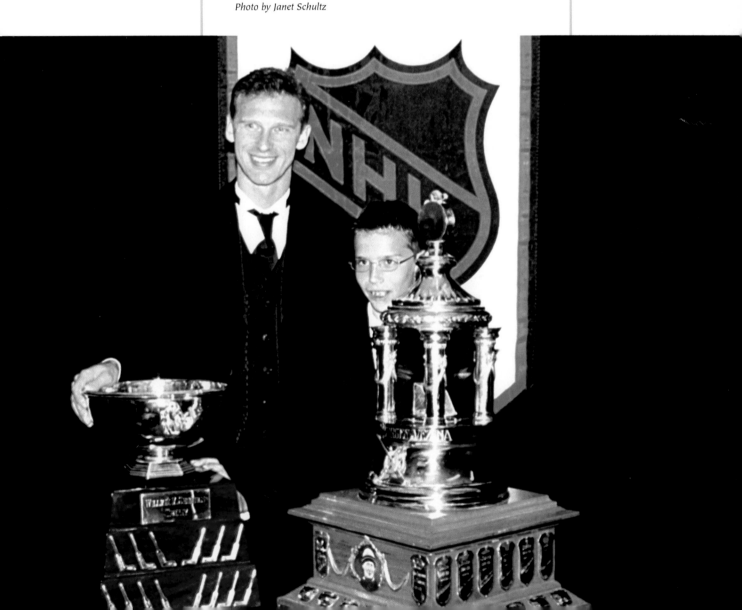

"We would gather around the tree and open presents. The next day was spent playing with our presents and spending time with the family."

Now that Hasek lives with his wife and two children in America during the holiday season, he still celebrates a traditional Czech Christmas.

"I send my children out of the room, light the tree with Christmas lights and not candles," Dominik says jokingly. "I still ring the bell for the kids and that's when they come into the room to open their presents.

"We try to call our families back in Czech on Christmas Day. But it is difficult at times because all of the [telephone] lines are being used and are busy. But after a while we get through. It makes for a great holiday."

As teammates begin to leave the room, Hasek says goodbye to the reporter. In turn, the reporter wishes Hasek well against the Sabres that evening. As he sits back down in his chair to remove his hockey equipment, Dominik's thoughts go back to his childhood.

Dominik faced more challenges on the ice than the opposing team. Here he tries to maneuver past Buffalo mascot Sabretooth.
Photo by Bill Wippert

Dominik's style was always to use his body to keep the puck out of the net, even in his early days with Chicago.

Photo by Bruce Bennett Photography

CHAPTER 2

Once a Goalie, Always a Goalie

From the time he was a little boy, no matter if he was playing hockey or soccer, Dominik wanted to be a goalie.

"I was born with very flexible legs," said Dominik. "I can remember that when I was about nine or 10, I could do almost a 180-degree leg split. And even as I got older, I really didn't lose much of that flexibility. What I do today is almost what I could do when I was a youngster."

And as far back as Dominik can remember, he was always a goalie. He admits that he basically taught himself to be a goalie.

"When I began playing hockey, nobody really taught me how to play the position," said Dominik. "My quick hands came from playing tennis. I played a lot with my brother, Martin. We played tennis a lot when we were kids.

"I learned to develop my leg quickness from playing a form of soccer outdoors. My legs were always moving. I learned how to go down, side to side, and even up."

Dominik admitted that he has always enjoyed playing goal.

"I was always the youngest guy on the team, and I liked to challenge the older guys I played against," said Dominik.

As Dominik got older, he continued to climb the ladder of success with hockey teams. By the time he was 16, Dominik was the starting goaltender in the Czech First Division. At 18, he was challenging for a starting job on the Czechoslovakian national team. And by the time he was 21,

Dominik was the starting net minder on the national team.

Soon afterwards the awards began to come Dominik's way. He was named Czechoslovakian First Team All-Star in 1988, 1989, and 1990; Czechoslovakian Player of the Year in 1987, 1989, and 1990; Czechoslovakian Goaltender of the Year 1986, 1987, 1988, 1989, and 1990. He represented Czechoslovakia as a member of their hockey team in the 1988 Winter Olympics.

In 1983, the Chicago Blackhawks selected Dominik as their eleventh choice (the 199th player taken overall) in the NHL Entry Draft.

"I really didn't know too much about the NHL at that time," Dominik said. "I really didn't think about coming to Chicago at that time because of the situation in our country. It would have been dangerous for me at that time to come over to the U.S. Had I left my country, I don't know what would have happened to my parents, my brother, or my sister.

"If I would have left my country at that time, I would not have been able to go back. I would have had to leave everything and everybody behind. I don't know what kind of harm would have come to my family had I left. We were under Communist rule at the time. Things were not as free at

Dominik played in 25 regular season games and four playoff games over two seasons in Chicago.
Photo by Bruce Bennett Photography

that time as they are today. The NHL was something I wanted to do at that time."

Instead, Dominik went to college, learned to speak English and Russian in addition to his native Czechoslovakian, and continued to develop his goaltending skills while becoming a superstar in the Czech Republic.

But life changed for Dominik when Communism fell in his country. In 1990 he signed a contract with the Blackhawks but was assigned to their minor-league team in Indianapolis, and he spent the 1990-91 and 1991-92 seasons bouncing between Indianapolis and Chicago.

He immediately found himself fourth on the Blackhawks' depth chart of goaltenders behind Ed Belfour, Greg Millen, and Jimmy Waite. Hasek also found out that because of league rules, he couldn't wear number nine, which he had worn for years in his native country. Instead he settled for 39.

Blackhawks headshot

Dominik guards the net during his minor-league days playing for the Indianapolis Ice.
Photo courtesy of the Indianapolis Ice

Indianapolis headshot

By the end of the 1992 season, Dominik was discouraged. Hasek's one shining moment occured in Game 4 of the 1992 Stanley Cup Finals between the Hawks and the Pittsburgh Penguins.

Chicago head coach Mike Keenan replaced Belfour with Hasek midway through Game 4. In just half of a game, Hasek stopped the Pens' Mario Lemieux one on one three times.

Hasek knew he could repeat that kind of performance if given a chance. Although he had seen limited action with Chicago, he wanted a shot as a starter. The Blackhawks gave him that opportunity when they traded Dominik to the Sabres on August 7, 1992 for Stephane Beauregard and Buffalo's fourth-round choice (Eric Daze) in the 1993 NHL Entry Draft.

But once again Dominik found himself behind another goalie, this time Grant Fuhr. But when an injury sidelined Fuhr early in the 1992-93 season, Dominik made the most of his opportunity.

The rest, as they say, is history.

Dominik's unorthodox—yet effective—style was
evident almost immediately in Buffalo. Here he stops
a shot on his back, with the handle of his stick.

Photo by Bill Wippert

CHAPTER 3

He Could Have Played All Night

"You knew the game would eventually end. You just wondered if you were going to get some kind of postgame meal or breakfast."

Jokingly, that's how veteran Buffalo Sabres right winger Rob Ray remembered the longest game in franchise history. It was the sixth game of the 1994 Stanley Cup Eastern Conference quarterfinal playoff series between the Sabres and New Jersey Devils. The game, played in Buffalo's Memorial Auditorium, took four overtime periods to play, with the Sabres prevailing 1-0 on a goal by Dave Hannan.

The sixth longest game in NHL history began at 7:35 p.m. on Wednesday, April 27. It ended at 1:52 a.m. on Thursday, April 28. It was a battle of goaltenders, as Hasek made 70 saves for the Sabres while Devils backstopper Martin Brodeur stopped 49 shots.

Dominik returns to the ice for another period of hockey on April 27, 1994. The Devils and Sabres played four overtime periods that night.
Photo by Bill Wippert

For six hours and 20 minutes, or 125 minutes and 43 seconds of actual play, the Dominator stonewalled every shooter New Jersey had in their lineup that night. He stopped shots with his glove, blocker, goalie pads, chest, feet, back, and yes, even his elbow.

"That game was one of my most memorable as a Sabre," said Dominik. "I remember a lot of the shots in the overtime. I knew the shooters were getting tired and that their shots would come easier for a goaltender.

"It was all I could do to concentrate on the game, no matter how long it was going to last. I just remember Dave Hannan scoring the goal and the red light going on. It was almost 10 minutes of two in the morning. It was nice to finally have the game over."

The man who scored the goal was relieved as well.

"I have a lot of great memories from my hockey career, but this one is really special," recalled Hannan. "I always played hard, and that's what I wanted to be judged on. I want to always be remembered as a player who gave his all for his team."

On the game-winning goal, Wayne Presley had started the play from behind the net. He fired the puck to Jason Dawe, who moved through the right faceoff circle near Brodeur. With Devils defenseman Bruce Driver clinging to Dawe, the left winger one-handed a pass into the slot area in front of the New Jersey net.

The puck hit Devils forward Valeri Zelepukin's skate and bounced over to Hannan, who backhanded a shot past Brodeur from about 12 feet away.

Sabres left wing Dave Hannan finally puts the puck in the net at 1:52 a.m. on Thursday, April 28, 1994. It was the lone goal scored in the Sabres victory over the New Jersey Devils—a game that extended four overtimes and lasted longer than six hours.
Photo by Bill Wippert

Dominik watches a shot go by against Calgary in March, 1996.
Photo by Bill Wippert

Above: **Dominik's 1992 headshot, his first with Buffalo.**

Photo by Bill Wippert

Right: **The scoreboard said it all in Game 6 of the 1994 Eastern Conference quarterfinals. After four overtime periods, the Sabres finally prevailed on Dave Hannan's goal at 1:52 a.m.**

Photo by Bill Wippert

"I had remembered being on the bench just moments before and thinking that if I got a shot to take, take it," said Hannan. "Don't waste the opportunity. So when Dawe's pass came at me I just swung at it as hard as I could.

"When it went in I remember thinking 'game seven.' We were going to game seven. Actually, I wanted to lie down and sleep right there on the ice."

What Rob Ray recalled most about the game was the postgame in the locker room. Looking around him, Ray saw a group of tired and exhausted hockey players. All except for one guy.

"The funniest part was that after we came in the dressing room, reporters came in and talked to Dominik," Ray commented. "They asked him how he felt. And he answered that he could have probably played two more periods.

"I couldn't believe it. Here were guys almost crawling off the ice, and here is the guy who played in every second of the game saying that he could have played two more periods."

Ray also talked about the save of the game that occurred in the third period. The Devils' Bobby Holik had picked up a Sabres turnover at the Buffalo blue line and went in with a two-on-one with

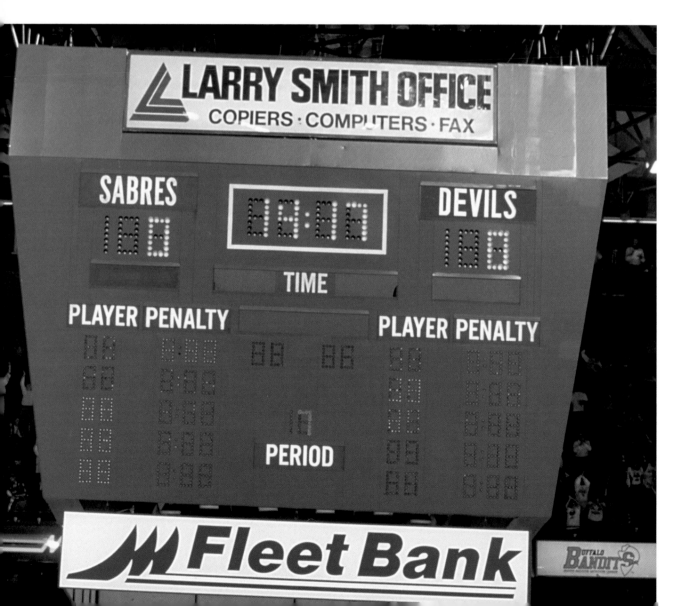

In the game that refused to end, Dominik makes one of his 70 saves.
Photo by Bill Wippert

Stephane Richer. As the two closed in on Dominik, Holik passed the puck across the crease to Richer, who fired the puck knee high. In a split second, Dominik lunged across the crease, did the splits, and grabbed the puck out of midair.

"All I know is that it brought the crowd to its feet and left most of us shaking our heads," Ray said. "You thought you had seen it all at that point. Dom was amazing.

"I know I've played in a lot of regular season games. But none will ever give me the feeling of excitement and the memories that a Stanley Cup playoff game like game six against the Devils did.

"The game and Dom were ones for the books."

In 1993-94, Dominik took over as the Sabres' number one goalie and led the league with seven shutouts, a 1.95 goals-against average and a 93.0 save percentage.

Photo by Bill Wippert

**Dominik foils the Dallas Stars'
attack during this 1997 contest.**
Photo by Bill Wippert

CHAPTER 4

Hasek Has Hart

"Dominik Hasek is the best goalie in the world."

That statement, made by Sabres general manager Darcy Regier, sums up what many people in the western New York area had known for several hockey seasons about their net minder. And on the evening of June 19, 1997, in Toronto at the NHL awards dinner, Dominik finally captured the award that has eluded many goalies throughout the history of the NHL: the Hart Memorial Trophy.

The annual award, selected by the Professional Hockey Writers' Association, is given "to the player judged to be the most valuable to his team." The trophy has been awarded since 1924. Hall of Famer Jacques Plante was the last goaltender to win the award, in 1962 with the Montreal Canadiens.

Dominik always felt at home in the net, especially in this January 1997 home game in Buffalo.
Photo by Bill Wippert

But when you take a look at the Hall of Fame list of net minders who never won it—including Bernie Parent, Ed Giacomin, Tony Esposito, Glenn Hall, Terry Sawchuk, and Ken Dryden, among others—it makes Hasek's achievement that much more amazing.

"Without Dominik in the nets for the Sabres last season, you don't know where the team would have finished," remarked Sabres assistant general manager, Larry Carriere. "It takes a whole team to win, but Dominik was the player who carried this team at times. He had a truly amazing season."

Award-wise, Dominik had the season that most players can only dream of in 1996-97. The Czech Republic native also won his third Vezina Trophy in four seasons, the NHL Players' Association's Lester B. Pearson Award as MVP chosen by the players, was named First Team All-Star, and was named MVP and Player of the Year by *The Hockey News*.

In 1996-97 Dominik posted a 37-20-10 record, five shutouts and a 2.27 goals-against average and led the NHL in save percentage for the fourth consecutive campaign. He also represented his club in the NHL All-Star Game in San Jose.

Not bad for a guy who just six years earlier was bouncing back and forth between the NHL's

Chicago Blackhawks and their minor-league affiliate in Indianapolis of the International Hockey League.

"He has one of the most unorthodox styles of play I've ever seen in a goalie," commented Hall of Fame defenseman, Harry Howell, now a scout with the New York Rangers. Howell, who played with the likes of Giacomin, Plante, Sawchuk and Gump Worsley, all Hall of Famers, continued, "But he gets the job done.

"Just when you think you've beaten him, he comes up with an amazing save. I have seen him stop shots with his blocker, glove, mask, and legs, among other parts of his body. He has done it standing up, sitting down, laying down on his back and stomach. The man is amazing. I've never seen anyone like him in goal."

Ottawa's Andreas Dackell scores on Dominik to put the Senators up 1-0 in the second game of the opening round of the 1997 playoffs. Hasek, who was battling a knee injury, would play only one more game in the series.

Photo by Bill Wippert

This 20-foot-high Hasek jersey stood in the lobby of HSBC Arena in Buffalo.
Photo by Bill Wippert

Dominik takes it all in stride.

"I'm just doing my job," said Dominik. "I've always tried to be the best at what I do. My style is my style. I don't see anything wrong with it. It's the way I've always played. If I pick up the puck with my stick hand, it's because maybe at the time it's the closest hand to the puck. I've just done what comes natural to me."

It is a style that helped him lead the Sabres to a first-place finish in the Northeast Division of the NHL in 1996-97.

"I had a very good season," Dominik commented. "I wouldn't say it was the best season in my life. But it was a very good season."

Dominik wanders the ice looking for his glove on February 19, 2001.
Photo by Bill Wippert

Buffalo fans knew exactly what they were witnessing in 1997.
Photo by Bill Wippert

He also knew his role with the Sabres.

"Every player is important, no matter if they're goalies, forwards or defenseman," the net minder continued. "I had never given that much thought to winning the Hart Trophy. The Hart is to go to the best player in the league. It doesn't matter if it is a goalie, defenseman, or forward.

"The [Hart] Trophy was never in my dreams. Of course, I've thought about it for the last couple of months [of the 1996-97 regular season], but before, I never even dreamed about it. It's the biggest individual honor for a hockey player. Everybody has a chance to win this trophy, but I was lucky enough to do it."

Lucky indeed. Hasek's name now joins those of past Hart Trophy winners, including Mark Messier and Brett Hull, both future Hall of Famers. Hall of Famers who have won it include Wayne Gretzky, Mario Lemieux, Guy Lafleur, Bobby Clarke, Phil Esposito, Bobby Orr, Jean Beliveau, Stan Mikita, Bobby Hull, Maurice Richard, Eddie Shore, Howie Morenz, Frank Nighbor, and the legendary Gordie Howe.

Sabretooth welcomes Dominik onto the ice in an enthusiastic 1996 moment.

Photo by Bill Wippert

Dominik trips up the Red Wings' Steve Yzerman early in the 1996-97 season. Five seasons later, Hasek and Yzerman would drink from the same Stanley Cup in Detroit.

Photo by Bill Wippert

"It is an honor to have my name included with players like that," Dominik commented. "This is something you only dream of. This is truly a great moment in my career."

His career has seen him gain the respect of the media as well as fellow players around the NHL. The Lester Pearson Trophy is voted on by the players.

"I didn't know I had this much respect from other players in the league," remarked Dominik. "I thought the award would go to players like Mark Messier or Wayne Gretzky.

"I was very surprised and pleased to win this award."

Lemieux recalls one game when he thought he had beaten the veteran goaltender, only to cut himself short of celebrating due to another amazing Hasek save.

"I remember cutting in on [Hasek] and a shot was fired towards the net," Lemieux said. "I tipped the shot and thought for sure it was headed in the net for a goal. But there was Hasek and his magic glove. I had already started to raise my arms in celebration of a goal. Instead I skated back to the bench wondering how he did it."

The smile on Lemieux's face after being robbed told the whole story. And Lemieux would not be the only goal scorer that Hasek stops now or in the future.

"I try to study each goal scorer I can," said Dominik. "I can only continue to do my best."

And "the Dominator" is the best. Most Valuable Player says it all.

"The guy has done it all for the Sabres," said Carriere. "He has been the backbone of this franchise. The only thing left for him to win right now would be the Stanley Cup."

Dominik fell short of that goal during the 1997 Stanley Cup playoffs when he injured his knee during the first round of the playoffs. The injury turned out to be one of the most controversial moments of Hasek's hockey career.

The Sabres were playing the Ottawa Senators in the first round of the Stanley Cup playoffs. Going into that first game there were a lot of off-ice problems surrounding Hasek.

Dominik (left) and teammate Michael Peca (center) and head coach Ted Nolan (right) share a happier moment at the 1997 NHL awards dinner. Despite winning the Jack Adams Trophy as the NHL's Coach of the Year, Nolan did not return for the 1997-98 season.
Photo by Janet Schultz

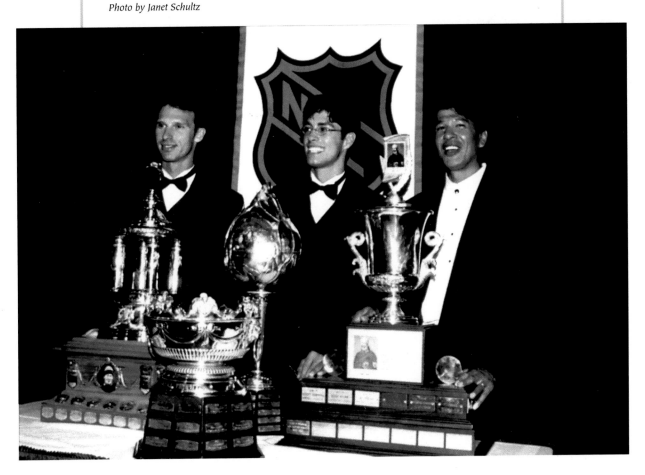

To begin with, the veteran goaltender was at odds with Sabres head coach Ted Nolan. Near the end of the regular season, Hasek smashed his stick during a practice at Boston's Fleet Center. He angrily skated off the ice.

The reason for Hasek's outburst was that he felt that Nolan was undermining him, behind his back, with his Sabre teammates. Dom also felt that Nolan was putting his ego ahead of the team.

In the first period of that opening game against the Senators, Sergei Zholtok of Ottawa crashed into Hasek. The veteran net minder suffered a grade-one sprain of the medial collateral ligament in his right knee. He immediately skated off the ice and didn't return for the rest of the game or series.

Surprisingly, Hasek spoke freely about his injury with the press after the game, something unheard of during the playoffs.

"I was down on the ice and just couldn't protect the knee," commented Hasek. "I never saw the player coming. I felt it crack. It was the first time I hurt my knee like this. I knew that I would be out for up to four weeks."

On top of that, Hasek paid a visit to friend Frank Musil, who was playing for the Senators but was out of the lineup with an injury. Hasek had been given permission to visit his friend by then Sabres general manager John Muckler.

Stories then began to circulate that Hasek's injury wasn't as serious as was being reported. The situation hit a boiling point when hockey reporter Jim Kelley of the *Buffalo News* wrote that Hasek was bailing out on his team. Local call-in radio shows added fuel to the fire by saying that Hasek had faked his injury.

At that point Hasek's temper got the better of him. Following another playoff game against the Senators at home, Hasek confronted Kelley in a hallway of Memorial Auditorium. The goalie grabbed Kelley by the throat, ripping Kelley's shirt. The two were separated by Sabres officials.

In the days following the incident, Hasek apologized for his actions. The NHL suspended Hasek, and his injury kept him from returning to the playoffs. The Philadelphia Flyers beat the Sabres in the second round.

Dominik knew he and his teammates had a lot to prove. And winning the Hart Trophy was nice, but it was not the end-all for the Sabres goalie.

The summer of 1997 would be a memorable one, not only for Hasek, but for the entire Sabres organization.

Dominik Hasek moves to block the goal as Brett Hull shoots the puck during the 1999 Stanley Cup final game. Hull later scored past Hasek in overtime to take the series.
Rick Stewart/Getty Images

Dominik hits the ice to keep the Washington Capitals out of the Sabres' net.

Photo by Bill Wippert

CHAPTER 5

Back-to-Back Harts

To say that the 1997-98 National Hockey League season was an emotional roller coaster ride for goaltender Dominik would be an understatement.

Dominik was a winner in several categories that season. He repeated as the Hart Trophy winner, the league's Most Valuable Player, and the Lester B. Pearson Award winner for MVP as voted by the players. He won his fourth Vezina Trophy, symbolic of the NHL's top net minder. In February, Hasek led the Czech Republic men's hockey team to a gold medal in the Winter Olympics in Nagano, Japan.

But more importantly, the Czech Republic native won back many of the hearts of Sabres fans around western New York and southern Ontario.

During the home opener, Dominik had been booed by many of the Buffalo fans on hand. The booing was caused in part by remarks Dominik had made during the summer over the coaching situation in Buffalo.

Ted Nolan, who had coached the team for two seasons (1995-97), was not rehired at the end of his second season. Dominik had made public statements saying that he agreed with the team's move.

"I don't believe in [Nolan]," commented Hasek at the end of the 1996-97 season. "I'll be happy if he's not back in Buffalo. I think in my heart I did a very good job for him. I didn't like the things he did, but the whole season I did the best for him and the team. I couldn't do anything else.

"But I don't respect him, and I don't want him back."

By the end of the summer of 1997 Nolan was gone, as was Muckler as GM. Lindy Ruff was in as head coach and Darcy Regier as general manager.

The booing continued throughout several more Sabres home games. Although Hasek admitted at the time that the booing didn't bother him, his play was not up to what it had been the season before. A *Sports Illustrated* article published early in the season even suggested that Dominik was letting in "beach ball" type goals. Dominik and the Sabres struggled throughout the months of October and November.

Then in December, the situation began turning around. The team played .500 hockey that month (7-7-1) and continued into January. Then a streak began on January 21. It was a simple 2-1 victory over the Carolina Hurricanes at home. Thirteen games later the undefeated streak (7-0-6) came to an end. It was just what the Sabres needed as they bolted up the playoff ladder.

During this time frame, Dominik's play also began to turn around. In the month of December the net minder tied an NHL record by recording six shutouts. He came within 19 seconds of six shutouts again in March (he finished with five). Hasek concluded the season with a career high and new team record of 13 shutouts.

Despite his slow start, the Dominator finished with better numbers than he did in his MVP season of 1996-97 (goals-against average of 2.09 to 2.27, save percentage of .932 to .930, and goals-against of 147 to 153).

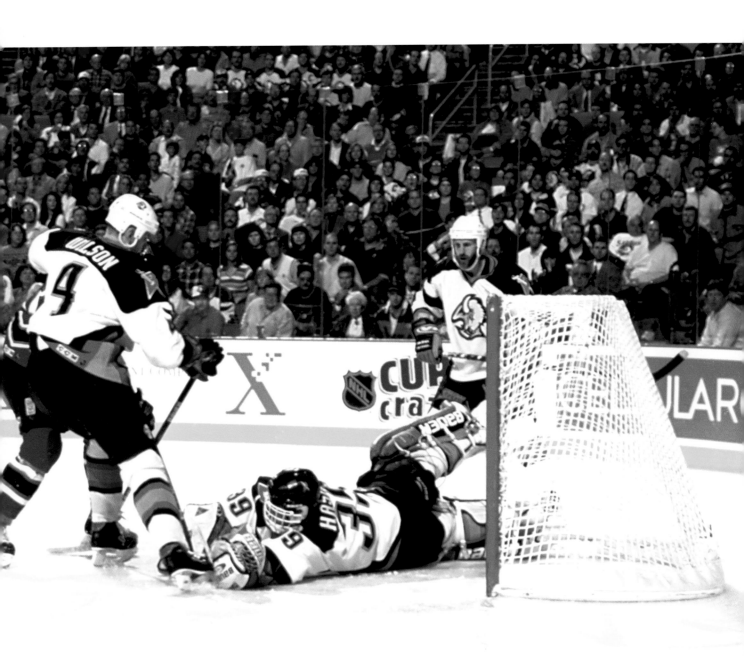

Opponents tried just about everything to get past Hasek during the 1997-98 season.
Photo by Bill Wippert

Dominik and the net never had a perfect relationship, as seen here in February, 1998.
Photo by Bill Wippert

Dominik continued his outstanding play in the Stanley Cup playoffs, leading the Sabres to series victories over the Montreal Canadiens and Philadelphia Flyers. Unfortunately, Hasek and Co. were stopped by the Washington Capitals in the Eastern Conference Championship in six games. By that time Sabres fans were back on their feet and cheering Dominik on.

And in February, during everything else that was going on in the NHL, Hasek proved to the world just how good he really was, leading the Czech Republic hockey team to a gold medal victory.

By the end of the NHL season, there was no doubt in anyone's mind that Hasek would again win the Hart, the first goalie in the history of the NHL to win it twice, let alone back to back. And one look at the Hall of Fame net minders who never won it makes Hasek's achievement that much more amazing.

Above: **Referees separate Dominik and Boston's Jason Allison during an April 1998 contest.**
Photo by Bill Wippert

Right: **At the 1998 NHL awards dinner, Dominik took home both the Hart and Vezina trophies—for the second year in a row.**
Photo by Bill Wippert

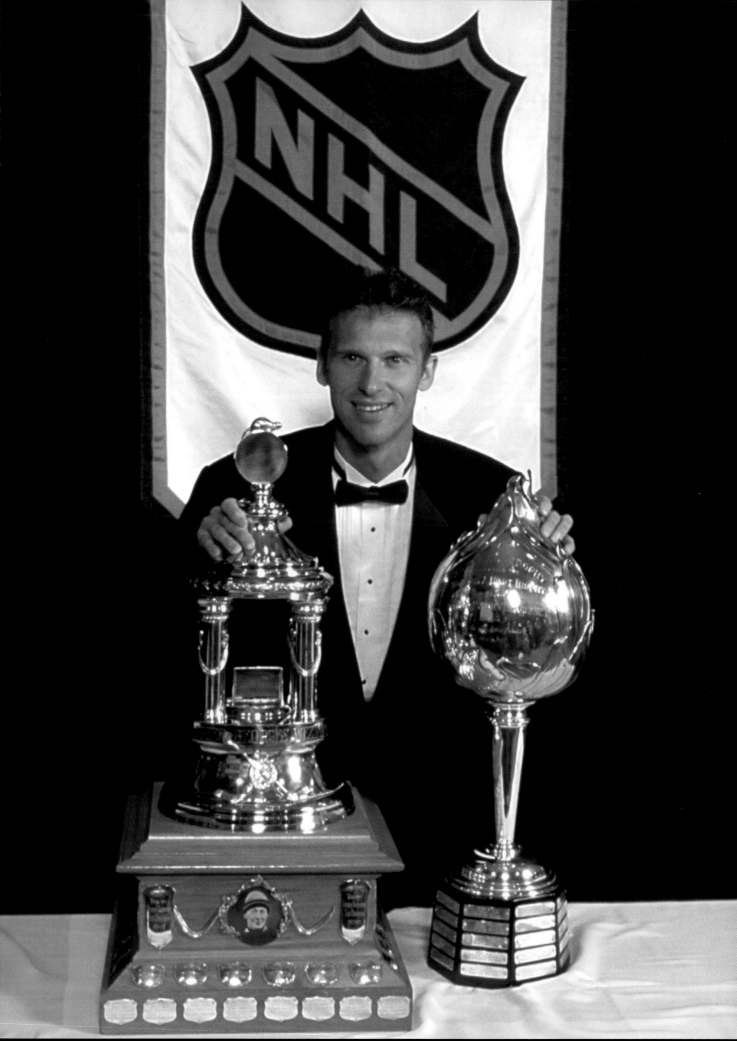

Dominik consults trainer Jim Pizzutelli during a game in Buffalo.

Photo by Janet Schultz

"I don't want to say this, but [1997-98] was probably the best season of my life," Hasek said. "You can't be happy when you don't win the last game of the year. I didn't go all the way with the Sabres, and I believe that I can play better."

Dominik certainly earned the respect of his Sabres teammates, especially during the playoffs.

"Dominik is truly one of the leaders on the Sabres," remarked Buffalo forward Dixon Ward. "Normally he lets his play on the ice do all of his talking. Or he'll say a few things between periods of a game. But he is truly the heart and soul of this team."

Even the Great One, Wayne Gretzky, admitted to the media that he thought that the best player in the game right now is Hasek.

"For Wayne Gretzky to say that about me, well, that's quite an honor," Dominik remarked.

Upon a visit to the Czech Republic, one finds out almost immediately Hasek's status in his native country.

"Dominik Hasek is God," remarked Paula Vlckova, a tour guide in the Czech Republic capital of Prague. "What he did for our hockey team and for our country is beyond words. He is truly the greatest hockey player this country has ever had."

But Dominik admitted that he had one goal left to accomplish.

"I want to win a Stanley Cup for Buffalo," remarked Dominik "I think we are getting closer to that goal. We fell short of that goal last season [1998], losing to Washington.

"I have always tried to do the best for my team and the fans. That's what I've always done, no matter if it is here or in my native country. I've always tried to be the best. I always try."

Hall of Fame goaltender Gerry Cheevers, who played and won two Stanley Cups with the Boston Bruins in the early 1970s, has seen some of hockey's all-time greats play between the pipes. But no one has ever caught his eye the way Hasek has.

"Hasek certainly leads his team by performance," Cheevers remarked. "He was a very deserving MVP for the two years he won it. There could have been other years that goalies could have won the award. But I don't know if it's the flair he's got or the uniqueness of his style.

"The one thing I know about Dominik is that he brings you out of your seat. He's a fabulous goaltender. Patrick Roy and Martin Brodeur are sensational, but conservative. But Dominik, he's something else.

"Guys like Hasek come along once in a lifetime. People go to watch Dominik Hasek because he is a performer. He's an entertainer. He is unique and the Sabres are fortunate to have him."

Canada's Eric Lindros tries to get his stick on the puck to shoot on Dominik during the sudden-death overtime of their semifinal match in Nagano on Feb. 20, 1998.

Frank Gunn, AP/Wide World Photos

6

Taking On the World

I t was approximately one month before the start of the 1998 Winter Olympic Games in Nagano, Japan. Dominik sat quietly in the team's locker room area inside Marine Midland Arena.

The Czech Republic-born net minder talked to a reporter about his home country hockey team's chances in the upcoming games, in which he would take part.

"For us to win a medal would be a great accomplishment," Dominik commented at the time. "But to win the gold medal, that would be my greatest accomplishment ever. I've always dreamed of winning a gold medal."

Dominik makes a save off Canada's Rod Brind'Amour as Czech defenseman Petr Svoboda covers during the first period of the semifinal game between the Olympic Czech team and Canada on Feb. 20, 1998.
Fred Chartrand, AP/Wide World Photos

A month later Dominik and the rest of his Czech Republic teammates made that dream a reality. For the first time in the history of the Olympic Winter Games, the Czech Republic won a gold medal in men's ice hockey. While there have been some hockey experts who have said that Dominik is the best goalie on the planet, after his performance in the Olympics, the whole world may believe that statement.

The Dominator led his team to a 1-0 victory over Russia on February 22 to win the gold. The Sabres' net minder certainly lived up to his nickname, allowing only six goals in six games, including two shutouts, with a .961 save percentage.

Led by Hasek's unique goaltending style, the Czech Republic team defeated the United States, Canada, and Russia in the quarterfinals, the three highest rated teams going into the tournament.

Just two days before their gold medal victory, the Czech Republic defeated Canada, 2-1. But the game had to be settled by a tie-breaking shootout between the two teams. While the Czech Republic managed to get one goal past Canada net minder Patrick Roy, not one of the five Canadian shooters could get the puck past Dominik.

The Dominator stopped (in order): Theo Fleury, Ray Bourque, Joe Nieuwendyk, Eric Lindros, and Brendan Shanahan.

"We believed that we could do a better job than at the World Cup, and that belief was the strongest thing you ever saw," commented Dominik. "If you could have seen everybody in the locker room before the United States game, the Canada game, and the Russian game, you would know that there was nothing more important.

"Our focus was very important and that might have been why we won the tournament."

Following the Olympic gold medal victory, Hasek was treated as a hero in the United States as well as his homeland. With the exception of Petr Svoboda, the entire Czech team returned to their homeland for a brief celebration. A throng estimated between 100,000 and 150,000 crowded into the Old Town Square of Prague, the capital of the Czech Republic, to greet their heroes.

Dominik makes a diving stop against Andrei Kovalemko of Russia during the final hockey match of the 1998 Winter Olympics in Nagano.
Jamie Squire/Getty Images

Upon their return to Buffalo, Dominik and fellow Sabre and Czech Republic teammate Richard Smehlik were greeted at the Buffalo Niagara International Airport by several hundred fans. And when Dominik and his family arrived at their western New York home, the neighborhood was decorated with Czech Repubic flags, and a group of neighbors assembled in front of their home to greet them.

"I was so surprised by the greetings," commented Dominik. "I didn't realize that we had this much support from the whole area or the city of Buffalo. I was really surprised when I found our neighbors waiting to greet us when we got to our house. This is really wonderful."

"I really don't know what else to say. I had a chance to play for my country, where I learned to play hockey. This was maybe my last chance to win something big for my country.

Left: Dominik celebrates with his team after the final match against Russia during the Winter Olympics in Nagano, Japan.
Doug Pensinger/Getty Images

Right: Dominik bites his Olympic gold medal after beating Russia 1-0 in the Olympic gold medal final in Nagano.
Paul Chiasson, AP/Wide World Photos

Dominik smiles as Richard Grasso, chairman of the New York Stock Exchange, displays Hasek's Olympic gold medal during a tour of the Exchange, Tuesday, March, 3, 1998.

Mel Nudelman, New York Stock Exchange, AP/Wide World Photos

"This is the greatest moment of my hockey career. To hear my country's national anthem play and see our flag being raised in triumph, that was a very emotional moment for me and the rest of my team. It is something you really can't describe unless you are a part of it."

Although Dominik was certainly a big part of the Czech Republic's victory, he still took everything in stride.

"We won the gold as a team," Dominik continued. "I didn't win it alone. It took an entire team to accomplish what we did. I was just one part of that team. Our country is very proud of us. They take the Olympic competition in hockey very seriously.

Dominik poses in front of his teammates for the team photo showing his gold medal on Feb. 22, 1998 at Big Hat Arena in Nagano.

Hans Deryk, AP/Wide World Photos

Dominik is recognized before his first game in Buffalo after the 1998 Olympics.

Photo by Bill Wippert

"A lot of this started back the summer before the Winter Olympics, when I was home. Even then, before I was officially on the team, people were asking me how I thought our team would do. And they wished me luck in the Olympics when I came back to Buffalo in August."

Hasek was also honored by having a stamp with his image on it made in the Czech Republic. Astronomers named an asteroid "Dominik" to honor him for the gold medal victory. And Dominik even got to sound the bell at the New York Stock Exchange.

Still, Dominik is surprised at the reaction of all the hockey fans.

"It was great, very nice," Dominik said. "To see the celebrations for what we've accomplished is something. We expected something big, but it's hard to describe in words what this has been like.

"I don't know how many people were in the streets of Prague. Maybe 100,000, 150,000 or 300,000. I don't know. I know there were a lot of people. It probably was the biggest event since 1989 during the Revolution.

"When we got back here we couldn't believe what happened, with all the people in the airport. Then there were 50 to 100 people in front of my house. The Marine Midland Arena was sold out, and it was very nice to hear the Czech anthem here before the game when they honored Richard and myself.

"I appreciate how the fans here have treated me. I'm still the same guy I was before I went to the Olympics. I haven't changed.

"But this is certainly be the greatest moment of my hockey career. I'm very proud of what we've accomplished."

The Czech Republic honored Dominik and his Olympic teammates with a postage stamp (above). Upon their return to the United States, Hasek and Richard Smehlik, his teammate both on the Sabres and the Czech Olympic team, were greeted by fans at the Buffalo Niagara International Airport on February 24, 2002.

Photo by Bill Wippert

With an uncanny sense of humor, Dominik could always put a smile on teammates' faces.
Photo by Bill Wippert

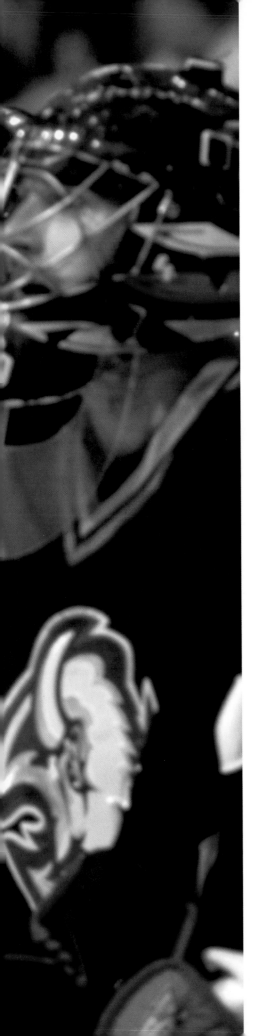

CHAPTER 7
Physically Fit

"No Practice. No Play. You play like you practice."

That is the simple message on a sign that hangs in Dominik Hasek's locker in the Sabres' dressing room. The sign itself is printed on an eight and one-half by eleven-inch sheet of paper. One has to step close to actually read the message.

In its own way, the sign is just a quiet display of Dominik's leadership qualities. The Sabres goaltender also practices what he preaches. Dominik works as hard in practice as he does during a game. There has never been a question of Dominik's leadership on the ice, no matter if it is during practices or games. There isn't a doubt in anyone's mind that the veteran goal stopper is the Most Valuable Player of the Sabres.

Distractions couldn't keep Dominik from his workouts, even in his first trip to Buffalo in a Detroit uniform.
Photo by Janet Schultz

If the National Hockey League would once again allow a goaltender to be the captain of his team and wear the "C" on his sweater, as it once did nearly five decades ago, there is little doubt that Dominik would be the symbolic leader of the team as well.

He takes his practices as seriously as he does actual games. The Czech Republic native works just as hard and stops just as many shots in practice as he does during a regular season contest.

"The guy drives you crazy sometimes," commented teammate Rob Ray. "Dom tries to stop every shot that's thrown at him. And he stops most of them. He is that competitive. He just never lets up. When we see how hard he is working on the ice, that makes us work that much harder.

"Believe me, I've seen my share of goalies who don't work hard in a practice. You'll never be able to accuse Dom of that."

None of this has changed as Dominik and the Sabres head toward the Stanley Cup playoffs each season. While some have expressed concern that the number of games Hasek has played during the regular season might tire him out, the Sabres coaching staff has always felt that the veteran net minder would be ready for the postseason.

"I don't think I've ever seen an athlete in better condition than Dominik Hasek," commented Sabres head coach Lindy Ruff. "Dom takes good care of himself, and he always seems to be in top condition."

Hasek himself has always been a stickler when it comes to exercising and staying in shape.

"Conditioning hasn't changed for me throughout my career in the National Hockey League," stated Dominik. "I'm still doing many of the same workouts and eating the same things today as I did before winning my two Vezina Trophies [1994 and 1995]."

Dominik went on to explain how he does his conditioning.

"I really don't do that much of it at home," said the Dominator. "It's even tougher for a professional athlete to try to exercise when we're on the road and in a hotel room.

"On practice days when the team is at home, I always seem to arrive at the last moment. The reason for this is because I always wake up at home at the last possible minute. So when I arrive at

Above all else, Dominik enjoys and believes in the benefits of stretching
Photo by Bill Wippert

the arena, I'm usually ready to go. I don't like it when I have to sit and wait around. I'm not that type of person who can just sit around."

If there is one type of exercise that Dominik enjoys and believes in above all the rest, it is stretching.

"I stretch before practices and games and between periods of games," explained Dominik. "I continue doing my stretching exercises before the team begins shooting pucks at me. I have always believed that goalies need to stretch more than the other players.

"Flexibility is very important for goalies, especially the way I play. Stretching my legs is important for me. I use my legs a lot more than any other part of my body during games or practices."

Left: On game days, Dominik drinks lots of water and juices.
Photo by Bill Wippert

Right: Stretching was always a part of Dominik's game-day routine, even in his early years with the Blackhawks.
Photo by Bruce Bennett Studios

In the locker room as well as on the ice, Dominik was a leader.
Photo by Bill Wippert

Dominik admitted that he exercises other parts of his body as well.

"I usually exercise my stomach and then my shoulders and arms," Dominik said. "I really don't exercise my legs that much, like lifting weights with them, because I'm exercising them a lot during a game and practice with the style of game that I play."

Doug McKenney, the Sabres' strength and conditioning coach, is the first person to admit that he has never met an athlete quite like Hasek when it comes to conditioning and nutrition.

"Like all of the other players on the team, I give Dom specific guidelines to follow for conditioning and diet, according to his weight and size," remarked McKenney. "I treat him no differently than anybody else. Dom keeps himself in good condition. He comes to me, I don't come to him.

"Dominik is very focused, no matter what he says. He comes into the weight training room after every game and works out. I don't have to seek him out because he comes in on his own. Dom wants to be in good shape. He knows he has to be. He's a very competitive guy and is always focused on the ice during games and practices.

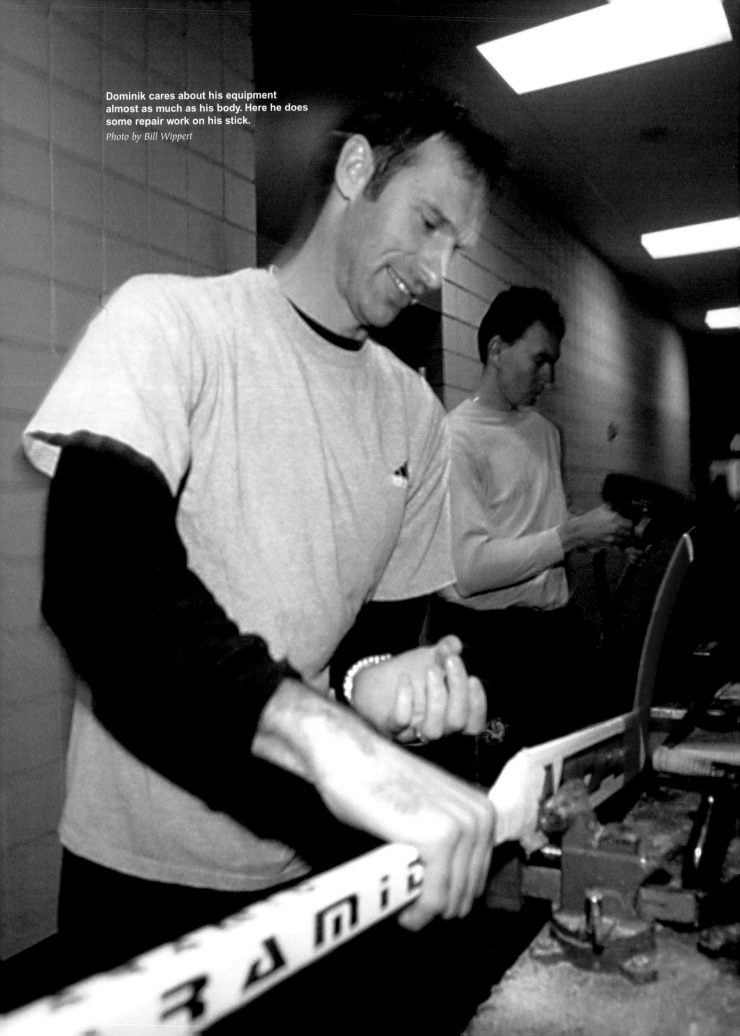

Dominik cares about his equipment almost as much as his body. Here he does some repair work on his stick.
Photo by Bill Wippert

"I may give Dom a guideline to follow when he eats and works out. I give Dom exercises to do, especially to protect the areas around his muscles and joints. He is so focused that he sometimes comes back and looks for new ways of eating and working out. He wants to keep that edge."

Just what does the Dominator eat and drink to stay in shape?

"I really don't eat too many sweets or junk foods," answered Dominik. "I really don't like sweets. I usually start my day with a big glass of water. My diet is basically made up of chicken and fish. I eat red meat or beef maybe 10 times a year. I also eat a lot of vegetables and fruit. When I'm on the road, it's usually a diet of spaghetti or chicken. When I'm at home, it's usually chicken and potatoes, along with some vegatables. I really like chicken.

"When I'm at home on game days, I will usually have a snack before I leave for the game. My snack is made up of a couple of slices of toast with jam or peanut butter on them. If it's not toast, then I will have a bowl of cereal. I also drink lots of water or juices.

"I'm very careful about what I eat and drink."

McKenney admitted that he has to be careful with Dominik.

"I don't give out any extra work for Dom because he plays in almost every game," stated McKenney. "If I did give him extra workouts, it could tire him out. You also have to keep in mind that goalies wear more equipment than the other players, which means that they carry around a little more weight with them."

McKenney sees the leadership qualities in Hasek and what he means to the Sabres.

"He leads by example," McKenney said. "I think Dom wants the guys on the team to be at his level of play, even in practice."

Looking at Dominik in street clothes, people are amazed to find out that he is a professional athlete. Hasek will be the first to admit that his weight hasn't

changed that much since coming into the NHL and has always been around 168 pounds.

"What is even more amazing is that I gain a little weight, maybe four or five pounds, during the season," stated Dominik. "I lose it during the off season.

"I know it doesn't make sense. But I've been successful, so I'm not going to change a thing."

Throughout his career, teammates would look to Dominik for leadership.
Photo by Bill Wippert

Dominik dives to the ice as Brett Hull's shot flies past him to win the 1999 Stanley Cup for the Dallas Stars. After the goal, many in Buffalo argued that Hull's skate was illegally in the crease.

Elsa Hasch/Getty Images

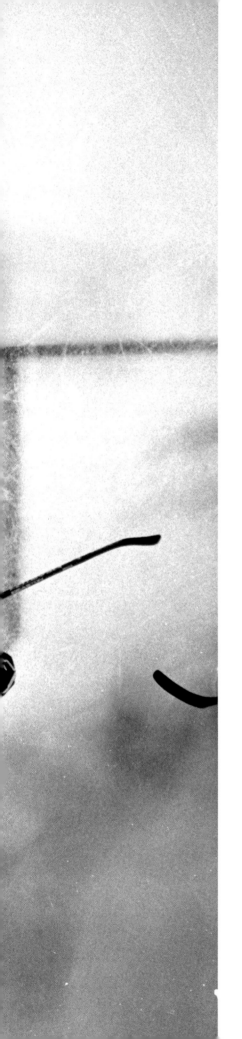

CHAPTER 8

No Goal

"No goal."

Those are the two words that summed up the Buffalo Sabres' 1998-99 season. Head coach Lindy Ruff used them in closing his speech at the team rally held in downtown Buffalo. That came two days after the Sabres had been eliminated by the Dallas Stars in the sixth game of the Stanley Cup Finals.

In that final game, Stars forward Brett Hull had scored the winning goal in overtime. The controversy occurred moments after the celebration began when it was discovered that Hull's skate was in the crease when he scored. Although TV cameras may have caught it, no on-ice officials did.

Dominik receives treatment for an injury during the 1998-99 season.
Photo by Bill Wippert

"There is no doubt that the goal left a bad taste in everyone's mouth as we headed into the off season," Dominik remarked. "After everything we accomplished and how well we played during our playoff run, it was a shame it had to end this way."

But even though "no goal" won't go away easily, life goes on.

"You would hope that we would all be back when next season begins," said Dominik. "Especially after everything we accomplished this year. That is something I hope will happen. We have a great team here. We showed the hockey world what we could do. I truly believe that the heart of the team will remain together.

"I love playing here in Buffalo, as do many of my teammates. I think we have a team that can win the Cup. We almost proved that last season. Nobody believed in what we could do last year, except those of us in the locker room. I think we have the players here to do it again next season."

And who would have believed it back in October? When the Sabres opened their regular season of play in Dallas, who would have thought that the same two teams would be facing each other eight months later in the Cup Finals?

The Sabres concluded the 1998-99 campaign with 91 points, ranking the team fourth in the Northeast Division and seventh overall in the Eastern Conference.

Many thought that the Sabres would pick right up where they had left off the season before during the playoffs, losing to the Washington Capitals in the conference finals. In fact, the Sabres began the season with a 15-5-5 mark over the first 25 games, tying for the fourth best start in franchise history. They were in first place in the Northeast Division through the beginning of the new year.

Then the team went into a nosedive, losing more than they were winning. Eventually they fell to fourth place in the division.

During the regular season Dominik had a streak of not allowing a goal to the New York Rangers in four consecutive games. And speaking of shutouts, with his season finale shutout against the

Dominik surveys the crowd with teammates Michael Peca and Joe Juneau at a downtown ceremony honoring the Sabres after their loss to Dallas in the Stanley Cup Finals.
Photo by Bill Wippert

Staying cool, Dominik enjoys the festivities at a downtown Buffalo rally honoring the 1999 Stanley Cup runner-up Sabres.

Photo by Bill Wippert

Capitals, Hasek had 41 career shutouts in a Buffalo uniform. He also captured his fifth Vezina Trophy in six seasons as the NHL's top goaltender.

Then came the Sabres' great run in the Stanley Cup playoffs, knocking off the Ottawa Senators, Boston Bruins, and Toronto Maple Leafs to advance to the Finals for the first time since 1975.

Unfortunately the great ride came to an abrupt end in the third overtime of Game 6.

"This team has nothing to hang its head over," Regier commented. "This team really came together as the playoffs continued.

"Dom proved that with a good team in front of him he could carry us a long way. His play at times was just inspiring. There was no doubt he carried us at times. And at other times he lifted others to play better. Everyone's play picked up during the playoffs. It truly was a team effort."

Ruff admits that he had his sights set.

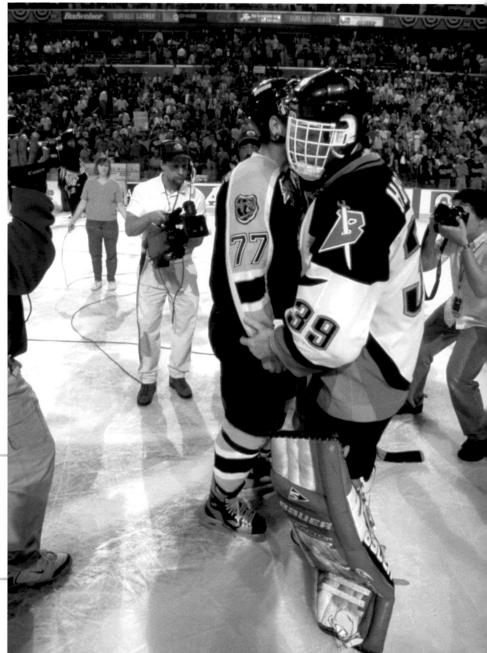

Dominik shares a word with Boston legend Ray Bourque after the Sabres eliminated the Bruins to advance in the 1999 Stanley Cup playoffs.

Photo by Bill Wippert

Dominik acknowledges fans at a ceremony in downtown Buffalo honoring the Sabres' 1998-1999 season.
Photo by Bill Wippert

"We were on a mission this year," concluded Ruff. "We knew we had a goal and that was to win the Stanley Cup. And, up until game six, we were on the path to doing that."

Unfortuately, it would be the closest Hasek would come to winning the Cup with the Sabres. While there would be more great moments for Hasek to experience, his next shot at the Cup would not come in a Buffalo uniform.

Dominik finds a moment of humor during a November 1998 home game.

Photo by Bill Wippert

After Dominik donated $1 million to local charities, Buffalo fans show their appreciation at this April 8, 2001 home game.

Photo by Bill Wippert

Dodge Different.

CHAPTER

First
Retirement

I t was a warm September day just prior to the start of the 1999-
2000 NHL season. Training camp had just started for the Buffalo

Sabres. Dominik Hasek emerged from the Buffalo Sabres' locker

room at the team's training site, the Pepsi Center in Amherst, New

York. Like bees drawn to honey, the media immediately gathered

around the goalie.

Dressed in a sweatshirt, shorts and sneakers, Hasek had not

participated in his team's first day of camp. He was recovering from

groin surgery and had been advised not to take part in any of the

team's initial training camp practices.

Despite his absence from the ice, Hasek was once again the

center of attention off of it. Only five weeks earlier he had

announced from his native country, the Czech Republic, that the

1999-2000 NHL season would be his last.

Dominik saves the puck with his stick while facing the interior of the net in a 1999 game against New Jersey.
Photo by Bill Wippert

"I think every game I play this year will be special to me," said Hasek. "Maybe some will be more than others. But it's the way I want to finish my career. And I'm not going to change my mind. I've made a decision."

Ironically, that would not be the first time Sabres fans would hear those words from Hasek over the next year.

"I thought about the way things ended," recalled Hasek, referring once again to the controversial overtime goal in Game 6 of the 1999 Stanley Cup Finals, scored by Brett Hull, which won the Cup for the Dallas Stars. "I thought about it for a week or so.

"And, of course, when people ask me about it I think about it. There is still the motivation in me that you always have to be a little bit better. Or that you have to win that last game of the season. You always feel that you can do something else. And this year I want to still try and do that something else."

At the time of the announcement Hasek indicated that it was his and his wife Alena's hope to return permanently the following year to their homeland in the Czech Republic.

The Haseks have two children, a son, Michael, and a daughter, Dominika.

"I can see every year it's more and more difficult, especially for my son, to adapt to the Czech life," stated Hasek. "Every year he has more problems to speak Czech. The longer we stay in the United States, the harder it will be for our kids.

"We want our kids to go back to the Czech Republic and share in our families' backgrounds and culture. When the kids are older, they will have the choice of where they want to live, but for now, my wife and I want to live in the Czech Republic."

And there was another major reason for Hasek to retire.

In Buffalo, Dominik did quite a bit of work for local charities. Here he entertains five-year-old Erin Deering at a Variety Club event.
Photo by Bill Wippert

"The attention I have received," added Hasek. "It's overwhelming. It's something I don't enjoy at all. I think there is a time to step back to a different life with less media and public attention. I don't want to live behind a wall. I hope once I retire, it will be over."

The problem would be, when would Hasek officially retire?

Hasek has accomplished enough during his NHL career to ensure him eventual election to the Hockey Hall of Fame in Toronto, Ontario. Besides the Vezina Trophy accomplishments, Hasek is the only goalie to have won the Hart Trophy and the Lester B. Pearson Awards twice. He led the NHL in save percentage six straight seasons and became the fourth goalie in league history with five first-team All-Star selections (Glenn Hall leads with seven, Bill Durnan has six and Ken Dryden, five.)

Left: **With a tear in his eye, Dominik announces that he will retire after the 1999-2000 season during a July 29, 1999 press conference in Prague, Czech Republic. After playing only 35 games, Hasek changed his mind.**

Heather Faulkner/Getty Images

Right: **Dominik walks through the tunnel towards the ice before his first game back from injury in February, 2000.**

Photo by Bill Wippert

Above: **Dominik answers questions at his locker following his final game in a Sabres uniform, a Game 7 loss to Pittsburgh in the 2001 Eastern Conference Semifinals.**

Photo by Bill Wippert

Right: **Even though he wasn't eligible (he wasn't born in America), at least one fan would have picked Dominik over Bush and Gore in 2000.**

Photo by Bill Wippert

Hasek also has an Olympic gold medal to his credit. The only piece of hardware missing from Hasek's trophy case was a Stanley Cup.

Unfortunately the 1999-2000 season wouldn't be a Stanley Cup-winning year for Hasek or the Sabres. The goalie missed 40 straight games that regular season with a groin injury. Hasek played in only 35 games that year, recording a 15-11-6 mark with a 2.21 goals-against average.

To make things worse, the Sabres were eliminated in the first round of the Stanley Cup playoffs by the Philadelphia Flyers.

By the end of the playoffs, Hasek announced his unretirement plans. He would return for one more season.

"I really felt that I didn't have the opportunity to finish the way I really wanted to," commented Hasek. "I was injured for half the season and really didn't accomplish what I wanted to do for the Sabres.

"I would like to play a whole season, healthy and without injury. Then we'll see what happens."

But the question did arise, "Just what would Hasek have done if he had retired like he planned?"

"I'm not looking at getting into pro hockey as a coach or GM," responded the veteran goalie. "But I wouldn't mind working with kids. I want to help kids, talk to them, educate them. Maybe I can help. I don't know exactly how. But I just know I can. I also plan to continue my work with charities."

Hasek established the Dominik Hasek Youth Sport and Scholarship Fund in May 2001 with a personal donation of $1,000,000. This unique fund was created to help underprivileged children throughout the city of Buffalo play sports.

"I'm also working on a line of sports and leisure clothing," Hasek added. "It is named Dominator. I have to compete in something, like I do in hockey, and I feel business would be something to compete in."

But once again, Hasek fell short of winning a Stanley Cup in the 2000-2001 NHL campaign, although he played one of the finest seasons in his career, winning a sixth Vezina Trophy as well as leading all goalies in shutouts with 11.

Although the Sabres defeated the Flyers in six games in the opening round of the playoffs, they lost to the Pittsburgh Penguins in seven games. The final Sabres loss came at home in overtime with the Pens winning, 3-2.

Would Hasek return for another run at the Cup in Buffalo for 2001-2002? He wasn't saying yes or no. But when he arrived in Toronto for the NHL awards dinner in late June of 2001, Hasek dropped the ultimate bombshell on Buffalo.

Hasek had indicated that if he were to play again, he would want to play for a team that was competitive and a serious Stanley Cup contender. Did he feel the Sabres were that kind of team?

"No comment," was his answer in Toronto.

Which was as good as making a comment to Sabres fans. It was the first inkling that anyone had that Hasek wasn't happy in Buffalo and that he didn't consider the Sabres a serious contender.

Was the Hasek era over in Buffalo? A July 1 deadline was approaching in which Hasek could be signed by Buffalo, be traded or become a free agent. Time was running out to find out that answer.

Always a magician in the net, here Dominik appears to make his stick levitate while the New York Rangers' Petr Nedved crashes into him.

Photo by Bill Wippert

Dominik watches the puck sail over his head during this February 19, 2001 game in Buffalo.

Photo by Bill Wippert

Chapter 10

Hockeytown USA

A great deal of mystery surrounded Dominik Hasek as the July 1 deadline drew closer. Many thought Buffalo held all the cards in the situation. They could sign him. They could trade him. They could sign him and then trade him. Or they could just let the June 30 deadline for signing the potential unrestricted free agent go by and just let him go.

There were others who felt that Hasek really controlled his own destiny. If the Sabres chose to pick up his contract option, Hasek could retire, especially if he felt that the team wasn't a playoff contender. He could almost dictate what serious playoff team he wanted to be traded to.

Buffalo Sabres general manager Darcy Regier was aware of the situation.

Dominik surveys the Buffalo media on July 1, 2001 after being traded to the Detroit Red Wings.
Photo by Bill Wippert

"I think it is very possible that this situation could go right down to the wire," said Regier at the time. "And picking up Dom's option on his [$9 million] contract is one of those options. And that could help in continuing trade talks with other teams.

"I think if you don't pick up the option, then you're recognizing that the asset [Hasek] is gone. On the other hand, nine million dollars is a lot of money."

Especially for a team strapped for money like the Sabres were. Considered a small-market team, Buffalo didn't have a large payroll, except for Hasek's contract.

In the days leading up to the July 1 deadline, Hasek was rumored to be going to several different teams including the Los Angeles Kings, Vancouver Canucks, New York Rangers, St. Louis Blues, and Detroit Red Wings.

The Blues seemed to show the most interest. During the NHL Entry Draft held in late June, St. Louis had traded their starting goalie, Roman Turek, to the Calgary Flames. The Blues were considered a serious Cup contender in the NHL's Western Division. Many felt that the only reason they couldn't go all the way was due to their lack of superior goaltending.

Many felt that Hasek could fill that bill.

Regier made it quite clear as well that if Hasek were traded, the Marty Biron era of hockey would be ready to begin in Buffalo.

"Marty Biron has already established the fact that he can play in the National Hockey League," said Regier. "He played very well two years ago when Dom was out. And he filled in quite well this year when called upon.

"He's ready."

Dominik bids farewell to Frank Henry, his good friend and the NHL's longtime security representative in Buffalo.
Photo by Bill Wippert

On June 30 all of Western New York waited to hear what would happen to Hasek. Finally the news came. Surprisingly, the Red Wings came in with a deal at the last minute. In exchange for Hasek the Sabres would receive forward Vyachesla Kozlov and a first-round pick in the 2002 NHL Entry Draft from Detroit.

"I'm very happy going to Detroit," commented Hasek. "Looking at the lineup they have and the players they have signed, they are a serious contender for the Stanley Cup.

"Plus, there is a lot of great hockey history connected with the Red Wings and Detroit. They have won a lot of Stanley Cups. They are constantly building a winner."

After winning back-to-back Stanley Cups in 1996-97 and 1997-98, Detroit had gone three straight Cupless seasons. Winning the Cup was expected in Detroit.

Left: **Dominik, shown here in January 2001, works with his eventual replacement in Buffalo, Martin Biron.**

Photo by Bill Wippert

Right: **Dominik meets the Detroit media during a news conference on Monday, July 2, 2001 after he was acquired from Buffalo for veteran left wing Vyacheslav Kozlov.**

Carlos Osorio, AP/Wide World Photos

After saying goodbye to Buffalo, Dominik gets into his Dodge Durango and heads to Detroit.
Photo by Bill Wippert

Detroit had a veteran lineup for the 2001-2002 season that looked like an All-Star team of Hall of Famers. Besides Hasek, they had Chris Chelios, Sergei Fedorov, Brett Hull, Igor Larionov, Nicklas Lidstrom, Luc Robitaille, Brendan Shanahan and their legendary captain, Steve Yzerman. And they were coached by Hall of Famer Scotty Bowman.

"I had a lot of good years in Buffalo," continued Hasek. "I'll never forget the team, the fans or the city. They have all been good to me."

Michael Hasek answers a question as his father looks on during a news conference in Detroit on July 2, 2001.

Carlos Osorio, AP/Wide World Photos

Unfortunately, Hasek was asked one question to which the answer would set off feelings of betrayal in Sabres fans.

When asked what uniform he would want to be pictured in when he was inducted into hockey's Hall of Fame, Hasek simply replied, "Detroit."

When asked to explain his answer later, Hasek avoided any further controversy.

"I came to Detroit to win the Stanley Cup," said Hasek. "That's all I want to do."

Of course the next question that needed to be answered would be how long Hasek would play in Detroit. A year? Two, maybe?

"I don't know at this time," responded Hasek at the start of the 2001-2002 season.

But Buffalo's Regier had another answer.

"Dom, in all likelihood, is going to play just one more year," said Regier. "It's always possible that he could certainly change his mind on that."

Regier summed up Hasek's pending retirement best.

"He redefined how the position is played," commented Regier. "He worked his way up from the bottom to be the best goalie on the planet. There is no doubt that by the time he retires he will rank up with the best of all time.

"Players like Dom only pass this way once. Enjoy him while you can."

That is what Red Wings fans expected to do in 2001-2002.

But he would only be successful if he led the Wings to a Cup. Hasek seemed ready for the challenge.

After the trade, Dominik returned to the Buffalo ice just once more—in a Red Wings uniform on March 10, 2002.

Photo by Bill Wippert

Dominik Hasek poses for a photo with a group of children enrolled in the Hasek's Heroes youth skating program. Dominik was in town for his first game back in Buffalo as a member of the Detroit Red Wings.

David Duprey, AP/Wide World Photos

CHAPTER 11

The Final Piece

"I won many individual trophies, but my biggest desire is to win the Cup, and I feel Detroit is a much better place—not a better place, but a bigger chance—to do that. I believe with my help and with the players and coaches over there, we can do it.

"Detroit is a team I believe can do it. I feel Detroit is more talented than the Sabres."

Those were Dominik Hasek's departing words as he left Buffalo for Detroit in July. Hasek had been disappointed when the Sabres failed to sign a veteran player for the 2001 Stanley Cup playoff run.

When Dominik returned to Buffalo on Sunday, March 10, the Sabres toppled the Red Wings by a 5-1 margin. Dominik played two periods and allowed four of the five goals.
Photo by Bill Wippert

Hasek had begged the Sabres to add a veteran player to the team who might replace Michael Peca, who had held out all season in a contract dispute. When that didn't happen, Hasek had had enough. He wanted out of Buffalo. He got his wish when he was traded to the Red Wings.

When he faced the Detroit press for the first time, he uttered the following statement:

"I am here to win the Cup. Nothing else. Nothing less."

The Dominator had a $1 million bonus in his contract if he won the Cup. But for Hasek it was more than just bonus money.

When the Wings opened training camp for the 2001-2002 season, their veteran roster resembled that of an All-Star team. In fact, there were some who were already saying that this Red Wings team may be one of the best ever assembled.

The lineup included players who are excellent candidates for the Hockey Hall of Fame: Chris

Chelios, Sergei Fedorov, Brett Hull, Igor Larionov, Nicklas Lidstrom, Luc Robitaille, Brendan Shanahan, Steve Yzerman, and Hasek.

The Red Wings came out of the gate winning. And they won consistently. So much so that they actually went wire to wire leading not only their division and conference, but the entire league. Detroit finished 51-17-10-4 for 116 points. They easily won the Central Division, finishing 18 points ahead of the second-place St. Louis Blues.

The Red Wings easily finished first overall, 15 points ahead of the Boston Bruins, who had 101 points in the Northeast Division of the Eastern Conference.

Hasek adapted very well to life in the Motor City. Individually, Hasek had an outstanding year in goal, playing in 65 games, finishing with a record of 41-15-8, a 2.17 goals-against average, and a .915 save percentage. He also recorded five shutouts. The 41 wins were an all-time high for Hasek.

Dominik protects the net during his first game back in Buffalo as a member of the Detroit Red Wings.
Photo by Bill Wippert

Never one to back down from an opponent, Hasek stares down Satan—former teammate Miroslav Satan (No. 81)—during his return to Buffalo in March, 2002.

Photo by Bill Wippert

Hasek, although pleased with his performance, was more impressed with the team he was playing with.

"This is the most talented team I've ever played on," commented Hasek early in the season. "I think we all came into this season with just one thing in mind and that's to win the Stanley Cup.

"It really doesn't matter how well we do in the regular season. It's what we do in the playoffs that's going to count."

Fellow teammate Shanahan agreed.

"He has not won a Stanley Cup," said Shanahan. "But Dom is determined to get to that point. When I look back at the other two Cups that we've won, I don't remember either of our goalies on those teams [Mike Vernon or Chris Osgood] making a difference.

Left: Dominik Hasek is surrounded by a group of children enrolled in the Hasek's Heroes youth skating program in Buffalo on March 11, 2002. Hasek started the league when he was goalie for the Buffalo Sabres.
David Duprey, AP/Wide World Photos

Right: On Sunday, March 10, 2002, Buffalo fans found themselves in a strange position: hoping the puck got past Hasek.
Photo by Bill Wippert

Dominik laces up his skates before heading out on the ice to skate with a group of Buffalo children enrolled in the Hasek's Heroes youth skating program.

David Duprey, AP/Wide World Photos

"But with Dominik, it's different. I've seen what he did in Buffalo and the difference he made there with the Sabres. He can win a game for a team himself. That's a big advantage for any team. That's why I'm glad we've got Dom on our team this year."

Hasek was the first to realize that the situation was different for him now that he was in a Red Wings uniform.

"It's a great feeling to be on a winning team," stated Hasek. "The game is all about winning, so I'm glad to be here. Our team has lots of offensive power with guys like Steve Yzerman, Brett Hull, Luc Robitaille, and Brendan Shanahan. We also have a lot of great defensemen like Nicklas Lidstrom and Chris Chelios.

"But hockey is a team sport and one player can't do it by himself. Every player has to do his job and work in the system. My focus is to stop the puck and play good in the playoffs. With the players we have on this team, if we stay healthy, our goal is definitely to win the Stanley Cup."

There was one major disappointment for Hasek during the regular season. It occured in February at the Winter Olympics at Salt Lake City, Utah. Led by Hasek, the Czech Republic men's hockey team were the defending gold medal winners.

It was Hasek's dream to win another gold medal for his hockey-crazed home country. Unfortunately, the Czech Republic team fell short of that goal. In fact, the Czechs lost a 1-0 decision to rival Russia in the quarterfinals. Hasek was upstaged by Russian goalie Nikolai Khabibulin, who made 41 saves in the game.

It ended the chance for the Czechs to win any type of medal. During his international career, Hasek had won the 1998 gold medal, four silver medals, and three bronze medals.

The Dominator was very disappointed in the way his international career ended.

"The disappointment is huge," remarked Hasek. "To be honest, I am so disappointed. But I am so proud of the way we played. Everybody on the team competed from beginning to end. I'm disappointed at one end, but so proud of what we did for 60 minutes."

While Hasek may have had a low in Utah, he had a natural high in Buffalo on Monday, March 11, the day after he returned to HSBC Arena for the first time since his trade to Detroit. Although Hasek and his mates had lost to the Sabres on Sunday, Hasek received a bigger thrill when he got to see kids skate for "Hasek's Heroes," the Dominik Hasek Youth Hockey League in Buffalo.

Hasek had founded the program with a $1 million personal donation the previous March. "Hasek's Heroes" is aimed at schoolchildren from low- to moderate-income families in Buffalo who would not have otherwise had the chance to play hockey. In the fall of 2001, 212 kids learned to play.

The after-school program at two city rinks provides transportation, equipment, ice time, and instruction for players, many of whom are underprivileged children. Many are from single-parent families and have emotional or physical disabilities.

"My son, when he was four, five or six, he asked me to play hockey, so he got skates, sticks, and I paid ice time for him," explained Hasek. "But I know there are in this area many kids who had no chance to do what my son did. My goal is to give them the same chance."

"Hasek's Heroes" is a multitiered program with four levels. There are Hasek's Wings, Hawks, Sabres, and Olympians. This year the first two levels, Wings and Hawks, began. Over the next two years the other two levels will begin.

Hasek is pleased to leave such a legacy in Buffalo, where he spent nine seasons playing for the Sabres.

"Community, friends, people who supported me, these are the things you can never forget," stated Hasek. "Even when I left, I wanted to establish something—this hockey program. This was my idea."

As the 2001-2002 regular season was coming to an end, Hasek, as well as the rest of his Detroit teammates, had their sights set on just one thing. A Stanley Cup.

It was the goal that Red Wings GM Ken Holland had set in motion the previous July when he introduced three future Hall of Famers—Hasek, Hull and Robitaille—as the newest members of team.

"The deal to acquire Dominik Hasek really set a chain reaction in motion," recalled Holland. "We made some moves to try to win over the next couple of years.

"Our goal is to compete for the Stanley Cup. You can't compete for the Cup with a whole group of 22- or 23-year-olds. I don't care how talented they are.

"We learned that through the early 1990s, when we had a real good young hockey club but had to learn how to win in the playoffs. That's why NHL teams try to acquire veteran players at the March trade deadline. Veterans have been through the wars, and you know what you're going to get from them."

Hasek had been through many playoff wars. But the pressure to win this one was the highest the veteran net minder would experience.

Hasek knew that the Red Wings had lost the previous year in the first round of the playoffs in an upset against the Los Angeles Kings. The sting of that loss was not forgotten by those players on the Wings who had been a part of the team.

Finishing first overall in the NHL meant nothing now. The 2002 Stanley Cup Playoffs were a whole new season. There was a lot riding on these finals. For Hasek and Robitaille, it would mean their first Cup championships. Hall of Fame head coach Scotty Bowman was shooting for his record-breaking ninth Cup victory. Hasek and the Red Wings were on a mission.

Right: **Dominik, shown here in his return to Buffalo, posted a 2.12 goals-against average in 64 regular season games for the Red Wings.**

Photo by Bill Wippert

Dominik knocks the puck away during Game 3 of the NHL Stanley Cup Finals against the Carolina Hurricanes at the the Entertainment Sports Arena in Raleigh, North Carolina.

Craig Jones/Getty Images/NHLI

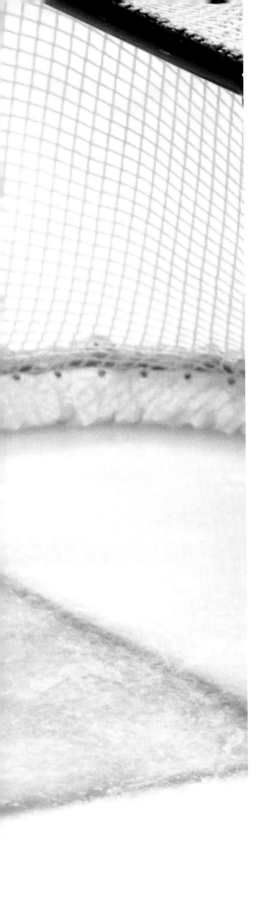

CHAPTER 12
Contentment

In the opening round of the 2002 Stanley Cup playoffs, the Detroit Red Wings opened up against the Vancouver Canucks. Finishing with the best overall record in the NHL gave the Red Wings home ice advantage throughout the playoffs.

But home ice advantage went out the window in Game 1. With the Wings playing in front of a jam-packed rocking Joe Louis Arena, the hometown team lost to the Canucks, 4-3, in overtime.

But a bigger shocker would come a couple of nights later when Detroit, playing at home, lost again to Vancouver. This time it was in convincing fashion, 5-2.

Suddenly Hasek was under the microscope. Critics came out of the woodwork, picking apart everything that Hasek did in the nets.

Dominik Hasek blocks a shot by the Carolina Hurricanes' Ron Francis during Game 3 of the 2002 Stanley Cup Finals. The Red Wings defeated the Hurricanes 3-2 in three overtimes.

David Duprey, AP/Wide World Photos

One thing that was noted by ESPN commentator Bill Clement was the fact that the Canucks had found a weakness in Hasek.

"Hasek has been going down early on some of the shots, and the Canucks are taking advantage of that," said Clement. "They're just waiting before shooting and it's paying off."

Despite the pressure, the Red Wings went about their business and headed out west to continue their series in Vancouver. And like they had done so many times during the regular season, the Red Wings focused their attention back to basic hockey and won back-to-back games in the Canadian city, 3-1 and 4-2.

By the time the two teams had returned to the Motor City, the Canucks were reeling. Detroit's defense was at its best in the contest as the Wings, led by Hasek, shut out the Canucks, 4-0.

It was a shootout, as the two teams returned to Vancouver for Game 6. But thanks to two short-handed Detroit goals in the second period, the Wings beat the Canucks, 6-4, to win the opening series four games to two.

In the next round, the Red Wings faced the St. Louis Blues. The Blues had easily beaten the Chicago Blackhawks in their opening-round matchup, four games to one.

Defense was again the order of business for the Red Wings. Detroit didn't make the same mistake they had in the opening round against the Canucks. In their opening two games at "The Joe," the Red Wings defeated the Blues 2-0 and 3-2.

Looking at a possible sweep, the Red Wings seemed to lose focus in Game 3 in St. Louis, losing 6-1. Once again, Detroit head coach Scotty Bowman refocused his team for Game 4. The Red Wings managed to hang on in that contest, 4-3.

Up three games to one, the Wings were ready to eliminate St. Louis in Game 5. St. Louis had lost their top defenseman and captain, Chris Pronger, to a season-ending knee injury in Game 4.

Although Detroit won the game, 4-0, the contest wasn't as close as it may have appeared. Led by Shanahan's two goals and two assists, the Wings completely shut down any offense the Blues tried to generate. For Hasek, it was his second shutout of the series and the ninth of his NHL career.

Dominik Hasek celebrates in the locker room after defeating the Carolina Hurricanes in Game 5 of the Stanley Cup Finals.
Tom Pidgeon/Getty Images/NHLI

In typical fashion, there was no celebration in the Red Wings' locker room following the victory. The Wings knew they would have their hands full in the next round. They would be facing the defending Stanley Cup champion Colorado Avalanche, with Hasek facing his rival, Patrick Roy.

In the opening game, the Red Wings came out flying. Led by Darren McCarty's three goals in the third period, Detroit beat Colorado, 5-3.

And like two champions battling it out in the ring, the next five games of the series see-sawed back and forth. The Avalanche won Game 2, 4-3 in overtime.

The series moved to Denver for Games 3 and 4. Home ice advantage again went out the door as Detroit came back to win Game 3 2-1 in OT. But the Avs would take Game 4, 3-2.

Game 5 went back to Detroit. Again, home ice was no help to the Red Wings as they lost to Colorado, 2-1. Detroit was struggling. Throughout the first five games, the Avs had scored the first goal of each game. And the Wings had not had a lead in regulation time since the third period of Game 1.

Left: Dominik Hasek lifts the Stanley Cup during the team's celebration rally on Monday, June 17, 2002 in Detroit. Hasek was prodded by the crowd to say if he would return to the team next year, but he only replied, "Let's just enjoy the moment."
Paul Warner, AP/Wide World Photos

Right: Dominik celebrates winning the Stanley Cup after Game 5 of the Stanley Cup Finals.
Tom Pidgeon/Getty Images/NHLI

Dominik shakes general manager Ken Holland's hand after his news conference in Detroit on June 25, 2002 where he announced his retirement.
Carlos Osorio, AP/Wide World Photos

Again, Hasek was under the gun, giving up two goals at critical moments in Games 4 and 5.

But Hasek met the challenge in Game 6. He was spectacular in the nets as he shut out Colorado 2-0 for his fourth shut out of the playoffs. The big turning point in that game, and possibly the series, occured late in the first period. Shanahan scored a goal on Roy with just 38 seconds remaining in the period.

Roy, thinking he had made the save on the shot, raised his glove. But the puck fell out of his glove and trickled into the net. It was all the help Hasek would need for the night.

Game 7 had all the suspense one would need. Many thought it would be close. Instead, it turned out to be a blowout for the Red Wings, who won the game 7-0 and the series four games to three. Hasek's shutout, his fifth, set a new record for most shutouts in the playoffs.

Once again, the Red Wings' celebration party was very low-key.

Czech ice hockey players from the Detroit Red Wings, from left, Jiri Fischer, Dominik Hasek, Jiri Slegr and Ladislav Kohn, toast with homemade plum brandy as they pose with the Stanley Cup at Uherske Hradiste, Czech Republic, Wednesday, Aug. 14, 2002.

Lukas Machalinek, CTK, AP/Wide World Photos

Left: **Dominik Hasek raises the Stanley Cup after defeating the Carolina Hurricanes in Game 5 of the NHL Stanley Cup Finals. The Red Wings won 3-1.**
Tom Pidgeon/Getty Images/NHLI

Right: **Detroit Red Wings owner Mike Ilitch listens as Dominik announces his retirement during a news conference in Detroit on Tuesday, June 25, 2002. Hasek wanted to become a Red Wing to complete his resume with a Stanley Cup.**
Carlos Osorio, AP/Wide World Photos

The Wings were going to the Stanley Cup Finals for the first time since 1998, when they won the Stanley Cup. Hasek and Co. were just one step away from their goal. Only the Carolina Hurricanes stood between the Wings and another Stanley Cup championship.

But as the series opened up, Hasek was again the center of attention. While on his way to practice on the day of Game 1, Hasek was ticketed for allegedly driving 65 miles per hour in a 45 mph construction zone on a downtown Detroit expressway.

Recorded on video and replayed on televisions around the world, Hasek didn't seem fazed by the incident.

Many hockey experts felt that the Wings would sweep the Hurricanes. After all, Carolina was the 16th-seeded team in the playoffs. The Hurricanes had finished 25 points behind the Red Wings in the regular season, the largest gap in the Finals since the New York Rangers' 27-point lead over the Canucks in 1994.

The series also marked the first time two European-born goalies, Hasek for Detroit and Arturs Irbe for Carolina, would be leading their respective teams into the Finals. No starting European goalie had ever had his name inscribed in the coveted Cup.

In the opening contest, the Canes upset the Wings 3-2 in OT, as veteran Ron Francis scored the game winner.

It looked as though the Wings might fall behind two games to none in Game 2. But thanks to two goals in 13 seconds by Nicklas Lidstrom and Kris Draper late in the third period, Detroit won, 3-1, to even the series.

Hasek was the difference in the game.

"We had a lot of these games against Colorado where you are hanging on one goal," said Bowman. "That's what the playoffs are all about. The edge seems to go to the goalies."

Game 3 turned out to be a marathon. Tied at two at the end of regulation, the two teams played almost three more full periods before Brett Hull scored with 1:14 left in the third OT period.

Seeing that the end could be near, Hasek and the Red Wings turned it up a notch for Game 4. Completely shutting down their offense, Detroit, thanks to goals by old-timers Hull and Igor Larionov, carried the Wings to a 3-0 win over the Canes.

It was Hasek's sixth shutout.

"This game was by far our best defensive game," commented Hasek. "The whole team deserved the shutout because it was a great defensive effort."

If there seemed to be one thing certain going into Game 5 in Detroit, it was the fact that the Red Wings were going to win the Cup on home ice if at all possible.

And the Wings seemed to pick up right where they had left off in Game 4. Hasek ran his shutout streak against Carolina to 166:03 before the Canes scored a goal. It began in the Wings' triple-overtime win in Game 3 and ran through the second period of Game 5. That turned out to be the second longest shutout time in Stanley Cup history.

With just 45 seconds remaining in the game, Shanahan scored an empty-net goal to give the Wings a 3-1 victory. As the final seconds ticked off, Hasek raised his stick and blocker in celebration. His mission had been accomplished.

Hasek had left Buffalo for Hockeytown, passing over other playoff-contending cities like St. Louis, for this shot at the Cup. Hasek's gamble paid off.

"What can I say, my dream came true," said Hasek in the postgame celebration. "It's why I ask to be traded to this organization, to play with such great teammates, great coaches. We worked so hard the whole year; all I can say it's a dream come true for every one of us.

"If I wouldn't have asked for the trade I would never have a chance to win it. I made the right decision and I'm so thankful to this organization."

Despite the pressure, Hasek came through when needed.

"We worked so hard to come from the first place overall, we used it against Colorado," said Hasek. "We played game seven in our building, it was so important. We were down against Vancouver, we were even down in the final, 1-0, and so you appreciate overcoming these obstacles even more.

"There's no better feeling than to raise the Stanley Cup. It's fantastic. It's heavier than I thought."

Obviously Hasek must have felt that his career was complete. Less than two weeks after winning Lord Stanley's hardware, the veteran net minder announced his retirement.

"I am and I will be a Red Wing forever," Hasek said in his opening statement.

"Winning the Cup has been everything I could ever ask for. After 21 years of playing professional hockey at the highest level, I do not feel that I have enough fire in me to compete at the level that I expect of myself."

Hasek's announcement followed that of Red Wings coach Scotty Bowman, who retired the night the Red Wings won the Cup.

"He left from the top, and I can say the same thing," continued Hasek. "It's a dream of many athletes."

Obviously Hasek's "Red Wing forever" comment did not sit well with those in Buffalo.

"We need to treat him with a lot respect," stated Sabres general manager Darcy Regier. "All of us who saw him in a Sabres uniform should consider ourselves fortunate to have seen one of the greatest goalies in the history of the game play. And he played the majority of his career here.

"And I believe that there will come a time when people will set aside whatever bitter feelings they have with him. I think time will take care a lot of that."

The only other achievement that Hasek can attain is to be named to the Hockey Hall of Fame in Toronto, Ontario, Canada.

With everything Hasek has accomplished, induction into the Hall should be just a formality. The only question that remains is whether he will go in as a Red Wiing or a Sabre. As Regier suggested, only time will tell how that will turn out.

Celebrate the Heroes of Detroit Sports
in These Other Acclaimed Titles from Sports Publishing!

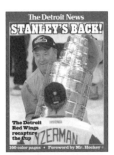
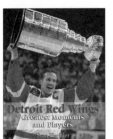
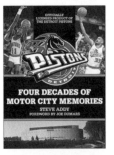

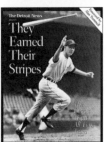

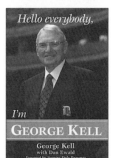